# Warrior Of Wisdom

---

## NO GRIT, NO PEARL

Building Resilience, Strength & Courage

### Helen Lauritzen

Cover, Illustrations and Interior Design by Helen Lauritzen.

All rights reserved. No part of this book may be reproduced by any mechanical, photographic, or electronic process, or in the form of phonographic recording; nor may it be stored in a retrieval system, transmitted, or otherwise be copied for public or private use – other than for "fair use" as brief quotations embodied in articles and reviews – without prior written permission of the author or publisher.

The author of this book does not dispense medical advice or prescribe the use of any technique as a form of treatment for physical, emotional, or medical problems without the advice of a physician, either directly or indirectly. The intent of the author is only to offer information of a general nature to help you in your quest for emotional, physical, and spiritual wellbeing. In the event you use any of the information in this book for yourself, the author and the publisher assume no responsibility for your actions.

Copyright © 2020 Helen Lauritzen

All rights reserved.

ISBN: 978-0-6487809-0-8

# DEDICATION

To my beautiful soul mate and husband, as well as my two gorgeous and awesome children.

Thank you for always loving and embracing my "weirdness". Thank you for *choosing* me . . . each one of you.

I am grateful for your love and support as I continue to grow on this incredible Journey. So honored to have such amazing souls by my side.

I love you all immensely. ♥

# CONTENTS

|     | Initial Remarks | 1 |
| --- | --- | --- |
| 1   | The Ancient Ones | 6 |
| 2   | Sweet Child Within | 11 |
| 3   | It's All About You | 16 |
| 4   | The Principles of Life | 20 |
| 5   | Acceptance is the Key | 24 |
| 6   | Believe in Yourself | 28 |
| 7   | Just Breathe | 32 |
| 8   | Signs Point the Way | 36 |
| 9   | Trust Yourself | 41 |
| 10  | Complete Harmony | 45 |
| 11  | Creating Your Story with Gratitude | 48 |
| 12  | Stand Your Ground | 52 |
| 13  | Sacred Space | 56 |
| 14  | The Light of Compassion | 62 |
| 15  | Somewhere . . . | 65 |
| 16  | Your Pearl . . . Your World | 69 |
|     | About the Author | 72 |

# INITIAL REMARKS

We are all on this Earth to be a part of a collective group, a collective Wisdom, a combined Soul. We have a lot to accomplish in order to undo the thousands of years of mankind's brainwashing that has been passed down from generation to generation and has been *accepted* from generation to generation without question, without denial, without refusal . . . until *now*. We as a race need to step up and clean up the old ways of an exhausted world, a world that cannot function properly any longer. A world that has crumbled around us and continues to crumble before our eyes . . . not evolving but dissolving.

We cannot close our eyes nor muffle the sounds of chaos and suffering any longer. We need to take charge of what is rightfully ours; that is a world that can provide as it once did so we can thrive in a healthy manner. So we can honor our bodies with healthy, wholesome, chemical-free and not genetically modified foods. So we can drink clean and chemical-free water so our bodies can then perform at their optimum level, allowing us to process our Wisdom and then progress to great heights, not in competition but in harmony and in support for one another as the *Ancient Ones* once did many years ago.

This knowledge of the *Ancient Ones* is weaving its way so delicately amongst the minds of many who are open to receive it. We are seeing a huge *Shift* around us, all over the world, a Shift that must happen if we are to continue to be a part of this beautiful planet that gives us Life, and is home to so many millions of fascinating and wondrous species including mankind. *We all* need to be a part of this Shift. *We all* need to accomplish re-igniting this planet to her former glory when Man was not consumed with fear and destruction. When Man was not obsessed with fame and fortune, with greed and frivolous objects of desire and power. This has been bred into and passed down through our DNA for centuries and has become heavily ingrained, turning mankind into unrelenting machines never satisfied but always wanting more. Always sacrificing freedom and happiness to have what is not necessary or needed. This is a trap that has developed in our method of thinking, a trap that has been set and re-set by the generations that have come before us.

We may not realize that we have fallen into this trap, this pre-set mode of thinking, but the evidence is all around us. So many people full of anger, anxiety or depression. So many people taking other people's lives and/or their own. This is the ultimate ending for many of us here in what was once a Garden of Eden. We have lost our way and have renounced our freedom. Why? We have lost our faith to be a united race that now continues to take instead of give. We have lost our 'knowledge' and even our love for one another, denying ourselves of freedom and happiness, not fully comprehending why we are here in the first place.

With all that said, this is not a book about what we should be doing to make this planet flourish with all that we need to survive, but a book that will help you to see that if we change what we have been led to believe then we will be able to take back what is rightfully ours and live in peace and harmony forevermore. A big statement to put out there? Yes. But the world is in big trouble and

**we all need to think differently to make a change,**

a change that has the potential to bring so much goodness to all those that hold onto a belief that this planet can be what it once was before we completely destroy it . . . and our selves.

We are lost to the knowledge of the Ancient Ones, a knowledge that used the gifts of the Land. A knowledge that helped us to keep a balanced relationship with Nature, our people, and our selves. Knowledge that included natural remedies, navigation by the stars and planets, signs from the Universe to follow our path and so much more. We have lost our internal sources of Wisdom to guide us in so many ways.

Nevertheless, this is not a book that preaches about the do's and the don'ts but rather a book that allows you to

### find the Wisdom within

rather than to be baffled and confused about what to believe and what not to believe. It is a book about going back to what was once a simple life of happiness and freedom where we all functioned in unison, using our individual talents and gifts to help one another and to live in harmony and fulfillment.

This book assists you to find

### your Soul, your Voice, and the Ancient Warrior

that is inside of all of us just wishing and waiting to be released . . . and to make a difference. There is so much potential in all of us that is constantly drowning in society's uniformity and conformity to think and act the same. We just need to dig deep within ourselves to find our *Soul*, our *Spirit* . . . our true calling, our Soul Purpose, and *believe* that we can make a difference . . . and create a huge Shift. Believe it or not,

### you are the maker of your World.

This book is about stripping away what is no longer necessary in our lives and reinforces how to be more courageous, resilient, self-reliant, but most importantly how to be *self-created* by accepting who we are to begin with.

Just like an oyster, when a bit of sand or grit enters its shell and starts to aggravate the mollusk, the mollusk uses its natural abilities and talents to take this grit, coating it with nacre, a pearlescent secretion, to protect itself and make a pearl. We too can be aggravated by people or situations that enter our world causing us grief, anger or fear.

**Like the simple oyster we have the ability to use our natural talents and gifts to protect ourselves and transform the negativity and drama in our environment into happiness, beauty, and tranquility . . . creating our very own Pearl.**

That is what this book is about.

# 1 THE ANCIENT ONES

So who are the *Ancient Ones*? No one mysterious. These are the Ancient Peoples of many countries, many nations that lived before us. A people who took pride in how they lived with the land, a land that provided so much in return for the care and nurturing it received from the people. A people that cared for and nurtured one another, always in constant harmony and balance with each other and the land. A people who could provide each other with a Wisdom so beneficial and empowering that there was no need for politics, hatred, and fear. They were people who, with their faith and wisdom, were able to heal themselves. A people who knew what it was to believe in themselves first, and not rely on the beliefs and falsehoods of unstable and unreliable entities that deliver false information. Entities that breed and thrive on the fears and desperation of those not strong enough to believe in themselves or in the goodness that surrounds them. Entities that feed off money, power, and greed.

There are small pockets of Ancient People that still exist today. Tribes that still live in the deep forests of the Amazon, Peru, Papua New Guinea and the deserts of central Africa. These people have courageously shunned the frightening and devastating outside world to keep their balance, harmony, tranquility, and Wisdom away from those who do not appreciate the beautiful world that they have.

These people have kept to themselves for hundreds of years, not wanting to adopt the ways of western culture so riddled with corruption, pollution and 'disease' on so many different levels. They are self-sufficient and content with everything they have, always living in the Now, making the most of what Mother Nature gives to them and forever grateful to be a part of a supportive community that encourages and respects each individual, nurturing their gifts and their talents.

Unfortunately, many of us living in western culture are not nurtured but dominated by the limitations imposed upon us. If only we, as a majority, not a minority, could just open our eyes and our mind to the endless possibilities that are presented before us day after day. We are constantly challenged and limited in our beliefs, in what we can and cannot do. We tend to ignore that Voice in our head, which is almost screaming out, and we continue to live in fear of what other people will say or do. Living in fear of humiliation and rejection. We cannot seem to think for ourselves, hoping someone else greater, smarter, richer, more successful (however *you* want to define 'successful') will provide the answer and pave the way for us when the road is *ours* to forge and create. We expect others to make our lives complete, to create our happiness and freedom for us. NOT TRUE.

It's a time of opening our hearts and our minds, just as we did when we were a young child, the age when we never use to doubt so much. We just followed our heart and did whatever it was that came to mind, a brilliant idea to try. Like feeling the movement, fluidity, and freedom of when we first rode our bike, amazed to be balancing and moving on just two wheels. Or completely submerging our head underwater for the first time and coming up for that next breath, realizing that you didn't actually drown, you were just fine, still breathing and still alive. In those moments, we proved our courage and our resilience. Moments filled with trepidation followed by bursting pride and fulfillment of achievement. We rejoiced not so much that we succeeded, but because we moved beyond our fear and took that step forward anyway. We believed in the *Wisdom* that just came to us with a 'knowing' that it was the right step to take at that moment. Most importantly we believed in *ourselves*.

Now, as we have grown older, that *soul belief* that we can and will achieve whatever we conceive in our minds has been diminished so abhorrently and aggressively by those entities that pride themselves and their successes (however *they* choose to define 'success'), feeding on the fear and lack of confidence in others, which they have continued to gorge upon for many generations before us.

We need to go back to

**the Believer and the Inner Warrior of the child we once were,**

never doubting but always believing that anything and everything is an opportunity worth trying and achieving. We need to start looking around us and living in the moment, the *Now*, which has so many answers and endless possibilities, making the road we are meant to travel, though bumpy and treacherous sometimes,

**an endless journey of inspiration, excitement, and adventure.**

We are beings of high intelligence and creativity, always developing new concepts and bettering ourselves. But somehow, within this western culture, we have lost sight of ourselves in the process, a process that has morphed into one of destruction and desperation instead of freedom and happiness.

Where has our Inner Wisdom and our courageous Child gone? Lost in a process that does not even serve us for our highest good, for if it did we would be truly free and insurmountably happy. How can we be free and feel this true happiness when we are surrounded by so many restrictions and so many decisions already made for and imposed upon us by others? IMPOSSIBLE.

It's time to break the shackles that we no longer should carry because *somebody said so*. It's time to bring forward our brave Warrior within that is just bursting to move to the front line and show us the way to happiness and freedom. It's so close to that final hour of change that we cannot ignore that Voice inside us that has been screaming for so long for you to listen. You know that Voice so well. It's time to remove the shackles and take your fingers out of your ears, hear what it has to say, Words of Wisdom from the Ancient Ones from long ago, buried in our DNA, just trying to break through and return us to the Garden of Eden that this planet once was. We just have to listen. We just have to believe we can do more to reach peace and harmony once more.

# 2 SWEET CHILD WITHIN

There is an ancient and interesting proverb that tells a story about "The Prince Who Had Everything – Buddha, The Enlightened One".

The story begins in the royal city of Kapilavatthu, where the great King Suddhodana and his Queen Maya gave birth to their son, Siddhartha. His name means "He Who Reaches His Goal."

Not long after their son's birth, the King was visited by an old, holy man named Asita who asked to see the baby. As soon as Asita looked at the baby he burst into tears. When the King asked what was wrong, fearing for the worst, the holy man said that he was crying for himself as he would not live to see this baby become a Buddha, an Enlightened One, and free the world from its bonds of illusion. He was sad that he would not live to hear his teachings.

The King became distressed with this new information because it meant that his only heir would turn to a life of religion. He called upon eight Brahmin priests, all skilled in interpreting

Signs, and asked them to tell him what future they saw for his son.

The priests had come to one conclusion which was: if the King's son follows in the King's footsteps, he would continue to rule the entire world. But if the King's son gives up his home and family for the life of a monk, he will become a Buddha and save the world from its ignorance and foolishness.

The King asked the priests what would cause his son to give up his home and family. The priests said that the Prince would see four Signs: An old man, a sick man, a dead man, and a holy man. The King decided to place guards around the palace to stop his son from seeing the Signs and all persons that fit this description were kept away.

As Siddhartha grew to be a man, the King used different methods to strengthen the prince's ties to home. He even married him to the lovely Princess Yasodhara who, in time, gave birth to a son.

Over time the prince became a creature of pleasure and seldom left the luxury of the palace. But one day Siddhartha wanted to visit a park just outside the city. The King arranged his outing, giving his guards strict orders to keep the road clear of the old, the sick, the dead, and the holy. As the prince passed through the city in his royal carriage, many people stood by the side of the road to marvel at him. The guards followed the King's orders as best they could.

But even so, the prince saw in the crowd a man with gray hair, weak limbs, and bent back. Siddhartha asked his driver what was wrong with that man. The driver explained that he was old. Not long after, the prince saw a man yellow-faced and shaking, leaning on a friend for support. When Siddhartha asked the driver what was wrong with that man the driver explained that he was sick. Then Siddhartha saw a stiff and motionless man being carried along by four others.

Siddhartha asked his driver what was wrong with that man. The driver explained that he was dead. Lastly, the prince saw a man with a shaved head and saffron robe. When Siddhartha asked his driver what that man was, the driver explained that he was a monk. When the prince asked what a monk was the driver said "a 'monk' is one who leaves his home and family to wander about, living on what he begs for. Avoiding pleasure, he overcomes the passions; meditating, he controls the mind. And so he strives for freedom from this world of tears."

At that moment Siddhartha asked the driver to return to the palace. He was not interested in parks or pleasure. "Soon I too will be a monk, renouncing this life that binds me", he said.

That night, the prince took one last look at his sleeping wife and son. Then he quietly walked through the courtyard and rode away on a white horse. Amazingly the city gate, which was too heavy for one man to open, had swung open by itself as he approached it. And as the prince passed through, he made this vow: "Never shall I enter this city again, till I've seen the farther shore of life and death."

Just like Siddhartha at the beginning of the story, we all tend to close our eyes to the many Signs around us that are prompting us to go in a certain direction, Signs that help us to stay on the right path and fulfill our Soul Purpose. We are pressured and so quick to listen to, and be persuaded by, others who think that they know better, who try to influence our path when all they are really able to influence and know is their *own* path . . . just like we can only influence and know *ours*.

It is our *Inner Child*, who grows to be a *Warrior of Wisdom*, who knows how to read the Signs, those loving hints we receive from the Universe that are all around us. It is our Inner Child that gives us that *knowing* deep down inside, knowing what is right for us and what isn't. This Child that we hold inside only has our best interests at heart. They are loving, caring and dedicated to serving our needs, making sure we are on the path that was always intended for us. They have no reason to cause us grief or harm. They are the sweetest yet strongest part of us, always willing to share their Wisdom, pushing us to be the best version of ourselves we could be, giving us the Wisdom to take the grit that is annoying us and to turn it into a *pearl*. All we have to do is listen to that Voice to know how to make our pearl . . . and believe. Believe that their way is the best because they know us best.

Perhaps you have seen the Signs around you and have experienced that inner knowing that they hold a special message for you. Undoubtedly and unequivocally they do. We will talk about these Signs later in Chapter 8, but for now just remember that when you feel that what you have seen and heard is a Sign for you then this is your Inner Voice, your Inner Wisdom coming through. When you follow that Wisdom, your belief in yourself escalates to greater heights giving you the sense of freedom and happiness that you had as a young child, because you achieved what you wanted. This is the Wisdom you need to follow. This is the Wisdom of your Inner Child which has come from the Ancient Ones.

Look around you and take notice of what comes before you. There is so much to see. There is so much to hear, feel, taste. All you have to do is use all of your senses, just some of the gifts you were given. Don't let the small and insignificant opinions of others shut your senses down. Sit quietly and open your eyes, ears, and nose. Allow yourself to feel the Wisdom coming through to you. It's *everywhere*. Stay in the present for that is where the answers are. Stay with your Inner Warrior, the Child who always used all their senses to experience and learn. Just remember every memory when you were a child, which brings with it all that you saw, felt, heard, smelt and tasted at that very moment in time, helping you to take that next step to feel happy, free and alive. This is the *essence* of Life.

**Trust your senses and know the Wisdom that you receive is reliable and true for it came from the *sweet child within* who loves you dearly, wanting you to survive and thrive, needing you to be happy and free.**

We come into this world with this Inner Child that knows so much. This Child has a sense of wonder, a sense of freedom that it wants to share. All you need to do is *listen*.

# 3 IT'S ALL ABOUT YOU

So we know there is always a part of us that knows deep down inside what we are supposed to do. This is the Voice of our Inner Child, our Warrior of Wisdom, speaking to us, giving us the answers we seek, and giving us the 'knowing' of the Ancient Ones.

**It is up to us to listen to that knowing, that Voice always nurturing us in the right direction, for it is this Voice that guides us the best.**

When you come to understand that this Voice knows what you are here for, that being your Soul Purpose, you will realize that you are supposed to continue your journey with this Voice by your side, always whispering in your inner ear to continue with your Divine Plan. This plan is the core of your being, it maps out your journey, your path, your internal drive and ambition to succeed and make a difference.

You will not always hear this Voice and often kick yourself when you don't listen to it, for deep down it is your *knowing,* your *intuition,* and it is always right. However, you can trust this Voice to the end of the Universe because this Voice is all about You. You are the sole reason why this Voice even exists. No one else, just you. It whispers to you only, pushing you to keep going no matter what.

**It's the Voice of love, compassion, support and most of all the Voice that holds the Truth in what is meant for you to hear.**

What we need to focus on is whether we are willing to open our ears and minds to the Voice within our very Soul that seems to resonate with our heart. This is the moment that we are satisfied that what we hear is what is *right* for us. We have to then be willing to *accept* it and move forward to action it. To hear it only is not enough. There must be an action that will bring us one or more steps closer to being the best version of ourselves that we can be, a person that can make a positive difference to ourselves, others and our world.

What we also need to focus on is our ability to be confident when we hear this Voice. We need to understand that this Voice can only serve our *highest good*, which means we can be confident to take action and know that we are moving towards a better life . . . and our Purpose. We should be proud of and confident with every step we take, knowing we are going to be successful and be the great person that we dream of being. We just need to listen to that loving Voice that is with us all our lives.

But for many we are so frightened of the next step, always doubting, always fearful of what might happen.

> *"What if the water rushes into my nose and mouth when I put my head underwater and I drown?"*
>
> *"What if I fall off my bike and break my leg?"*
>
> *"What if my friends laugh at me when they find out I love to go to drama class?"*

We are always wondering "What if . . . ?" when we should be saying "I can . . ." and "I will . . ." and with conviction because listening to our Voice and following our heart brings us closer to becoming what and who we are truly meant to be. This is when we start to fly, feeling free and at our best, continuing to move up another step on the ladder of our journey.

We are capable of so much if we choose the right *thoughts* and hold in our mind, and in our heart, the right and superior beliefs about what we can achieve in this lifetime. We are able to contribute to our outcome by the *beliefs* we hold in our heart. If we carry *limiting* beliefs that say we can't achieve something then there is an obstacle we have put in front of ourselves that is blocking our chance of making that thing, that goal, achievable.

> "I'm not a fish. I don't have gills. I'll never be able to put my head underwater let alone swim."
>
> "I can't balance and control this bike. I'm afraid I will go too fast then crash and hurt myself very badly."
>
> "I can't let my friends know that I go to drama class. They will laugh so much and I'll be humiliated."
>
> "What if my parents get angry or upset because I want to be a chef, not a lawyer or doctor?"

If we change our thoughts to positive and successful thoughts, minus the opinions of others, this enables us to see the vision of achieving that thing or goal. Then the obstacle has now been removed and we are so much closer to making that goal a reality.

> "If I put my head underwater I am one step closer to being able to swim . . . and a step closer to becoming an Olympic gold medalist!"
>
> "If I continue to try to balance and pedal my bike I am one step closer to riding a bike . . . and a step closer to being able to compete in the 'Tour de France'!"
>
> "If I continue drama lessons it will give me confidence and I'll be one step closer to being on stage in front of lots of people . . .

and one step closer to being a professional actor with a role in an amazing movie!"

"If I can just be honest with my parents and follow my passion for cooking . . . I will be one step closer to owning my own 5-star restaurant!"

**It all stems from just *a thought*, a thought that will either limit you or a thought that will make you fly to great heights.**

The difference lies within the *choice* that you ultimately make as to whether you believe that you *can't* or whether you believe that you *really can*.

Your mind has so much power to shape the path that lies before you. And the wonderful thing is that your inner Voice can help you make that choice to believe that you *can* so that you can be who you are meant to be . . . You.

At the end of the day, *it's all about you*. You are the keeper of your heart and Soul. You are the maker or breaker of your happiness and your life. You have the power to create a story that is so magnificent and all you need to do is listen to the Voice of that Child, that growing Warrior of Wisdom within that carries so much Wisdom from the Ancient Ones, the ones that hold the *keys of survival*, happiness, and freedom from long ago. The Ones that know how to *take the grit and make a Pearl*.

# 4 THE PRINCIPLES OF LIFE

There are so many unwritten and implied rules and regulations that society and organizations impose on us every day in all that we do; so many to limit us in how we think and how we grow. We have always been pushed or persuaded by different people who play an important part in our lives such as our parents, our teachers, our friends, our bosses, religious figures, politicians and the list goes on. They impose so many rules, where some are for our benefit such as safety and hygiene. Then there are other imposed rules, such as those created to take some action that makes us feel uncomfortable to some degree.

"You need to hang out with our group or you will be a loser if you don't."

"You need to go to Law School otherwise you are going to be a failure."

"You need to get a great result by the end of the month or else you will be fired."

Such imposed rules are usually based on an assortment of unsubstantiated opinions, to give these others a sense of 'control' over you, especially when faced with a "Do this or else . . ." ultimatum. This, in turn, gives you a false sense of 'belonging' and 'acceptance' if you do abide by them. These imposed rules can then be a huge hindrance to our *self-belief* and the Wisdom of the Ancient Ones. To stifle their Wisdom is to stifle our ability to follow our path, a path that will lead us to our 'true' place of belonging and acceptance.

To travel on our path there are *no rules* but a few principles, or guidelines, that we need to follow and they are very simple and altruistic.

The first principle is the *Principle of Survival.* This is the first principle because it is vital to make sure that you give to yourself what is needed to ensure survival at all times, such as food, water, and shelter for the basic requirements. This does not mean to break the laws of society for to do so will ultimately result in negative consequences. However, you do need to make sure that you give to yourself in self-preservation, especially making sure that you don't continually please others, and making sure you set *boundaries* to shield yourself during times of uncertainty which includes having to say 'No'. When your inner Voice is saying 'No' this *needs* to be actioned.

There will be times when your assistance will be needed by others but there will be times when you will need to step back and take care of what you need first, even if it means you need to give time to yourself and do nothing but rest. Even doing nothing is in line with principle number 1 to assist with your need to survive. This principle is foremost and essential to your existence and wellbeing. This is your primary obligation to your Soul and to your Inner Child who needs to not only be nourished but to rest regularly.

The second principle is the *Principle of Compassion.* Just as it is important to project love to others, this projection is much more than just a feeling or saying "I love you". It is a love that is unconditional and is embedded within compassion and kindness, to yourself foremost, and this then becomes a ripple effect that transfers to others. *Compassion* enables us to understand ourselves as much as it enables us to understand those that we interact with, not only on a daily basis but those that pass us for a fleeting moment such as the unhappy shop assistant, a stranger that whines in the cue, or someone that that is rude to you at school or at work. These people also require compassion, even when they seem rude and grumpy. And so do we from those we interact with. It is the people who are so negative in their behavior that require the most compassion for the path they have been traveling has been a bumpy and uncomfortable one for some time. It's up to us to reach out and offer positive thoughts and actions, as difficult as it may be sometimes to do something that will ease their path.

*Compassion* is the essence of our existence and is the key to *understanding*, and understanding is the key to *patience* and *tolerance*, which then leads to *kindness*. Compassion is a critical enzyme that starts a beautiful chain reaction of goodness and happiness, a massive ripple effect that humbles each of us. It is also the foundation of the third principle.

The third principle is the *Principle of Forgiveness*. It is important to forgive those who have wronged us. To hold onto anger and animosity is a burden so heavy it causes unnecessary turmoil and hardship, not only to others but mostly to ourselves. It defies both principles number 1 (Survival) and number 2 (Compassion) if we hold onto resentment and anger. We deny ourselves the idea of giving what we need to ourselves for survival including peace and harmony. We deny ourselves and others the beautiful chain reaction that starts with compassion and ends with kindness.

So it is very important that we forgive. However, this does not mean we forget, for again we are breaking principle number 1 with setting those boundaries that allow us to say 'No', especially when our Voice is saying or screaming that this person or situation is likely to control, upset or harm us once again.

Forgiveness allows us to free ourselves from another's negativity and hurtful actions, for to keep it inside only causes us anguish, pain, anxiety, fear or anger - all negative emotions that do not serve our Purpose but block it due to all the negativity we accumulate inside us. We need to clear ourselves of all negative emotions to continue with a positive outlook, a positive vibration, which continually allows us to attract more goodness into our lives. Simply put: "Like attracts like". To forgive means to release all negativity not worth carrying. This, in turn, opens the door and empties the space to be filled with goodness and positivity instead, therefore attracting more goodness and positivity.

Principle number 4 is the greatest and most conducive rule to our being and our Purpose. This principle is the *Principle of Acceptance*. Acceptance is a huge part of who we are and what we are all about. Acceptance unites all the parts that we are to make us 'whole'. We cannot thrive if we reject ourselves so there has to be total acceptance of every part, at every level, for it becomes a miserable existence if we continually *reject* ourselves instead of *accept* ourselves.

There are so many parts to just one person and the combination of these parts makes each and every one of us *unique*. This uniqueness helps the human race to evolve, making us very dynamic as a species, always striving to be the best we can be. To do this, we need to acknowledge our strengths as well as our weaknesses, which we may or may not develop further, it all depends on what we want to *see* and acknowledge, therefore what we want to *accept*.

It is this last principle that needs to be explored and explained further so that we can understand ourselves better, enabling us to hear the Voice of the Ancient One and the Inner Child . . . the Ying and Yang of our Soul.

# 5 ACCEPTANCE IS THE KEY

Acceptance is by far the most important factor to our entire being. This one word is the key to a positive, happy and free existence . . . an existence free of other people's opinions and hurtful statements that have no bearing on your Purpose, especially when you embrace acceptance of all that you are.

It's not about what you look like and it certainly isn't about how others *see* you or even *accept* you into their circle. Acceptance is all about *how you see yourself* and *how you love yourself* . . . the good parts and the seemingly not so good parts. And the word 'seemingly' is used because sometimes the not so good parts are based on other people's opinions which, quite often, are tainted by even more people's opinions and so on; a ripple effect of assumed opinions. These opinions, which are merely just that . . . an *opinion* . . . DO NOT define who we are. Only we have the power to define who we are. Only we have the power to see ourselves and to know ourselves the best, for we have all the answers inside us to follow the one main path that was meant for us only.

All that we are is a combination of parts that are specifically there to help us travel that path. These parts are our tools given to us by the Universe, Source or God, or whatever your beliefs. These tools are our gifts to share. No one else can give them to you nor can anyone take them away. They are always yours and will always be a part of you whether you choose to acknowledge them, whether you choose to accept them . . . or not. They are there from the moment we are born into this world, ready to use and to be accepted so we can grow to be our finest and most advantageous self.

The key is to listen to that Voice, over all other voices uttering constant opinions, and tune into its Wisdom and accept this Wisdom which comes from a good place . . . your Soul. This is the Truth which you can sense in your heart but, most importantly, in your gut for this is the barometer of your Wisdom which allows you to carry out the important factor of Acceptance.

Our gut instinct, our 'knowing', all happens in our solar plexus which is also the same place where we find our power, where we gather up "the guts" to do something. It is designed to filter the good opinions from the bad, regulating the information that we accept or reject. Most importantly it works hand in hand with the Voice of our Ancient One. A strong team of reasoning, acceptance, rejection, and power to follow our path, all working together.

**Acceptance is all about finding out who you are
and staying true to who you are.**

We have so many different parts that make us whole. No part is more important than the other. They all fit together like a puzzle. Different parts of the puzzle have different shades of light and dark, are large or small, some seemingly more special than others. However, every part has an integral role in making the big picture, to make us whole, to make us who we are. This is why it is so important to accept *every* part of us otherwise we are left with pieces missing, with holes in our existence . . . feeling *incomplete*.

We cannot be complete if we don't accept all parts that belong solely to ourselves – our talents, our gifts, our strengths, our so-called weaknesses, and flaws. Each part is connected to our uniqueness which, in turn, governs our Soul Purpose.

This one key principle, Acceptance, is what we need to embrace on so many different levels. It teaches us to stay true to who we are and to accept others as well.

**It is a universal principle that reduces resistance, opens our heart and allows the Wisdom to flow, increasing our connection within ourselves and the inter-connectedness with one another.**

By accepting all our parts we are more confident to show *all* of who we really are. No lies, no false masks . . . and *no pretending*. We can live life openly, enjoying what we love most, not afraid to bare and share our Soul. We can be vulnerable without shame or fear, for if we accept our self confidently, without guilt or humiliation, we have no need for the insignificant opinions of others which become impervious to penetrating our tough outer shell.

**So the more we accept who we are,
the more resilient our outer shell becomes.**

Again, we have the choice to say 'Yes' or 'No' to what opinions we choose to ignore and what opinions we allow inside. That is, what we accept as part of ourselves, what we ultimately believe and what becomes our Truth.

It is also important to spread our acceptance from ourselves to others who are also striving to be the best version of themself, so they too can establish their personal uniqueness and personal acceptance. When acceptance spreads from one to another, like a ripple effect, it takes us back to principles 2 (Compassion) and 3 (Forgiveness). These principles become well integrated, working together in unison and also allowing us to work in unison for the highest good of mankind.

# 6 BELIEVE IN YOURSELF

We all want to be confident, indestructible and successful in reaching our goals, our dreams. We have to constantly face failure and re-evaluate our plan of attack, continually assessing all factors presented to us daily. There is so much to take in, assess and evaluate. Choices, choices and more choices to be made, some more daunting than others.

We cannot always find a solution or make a decision. There is always some part of us that is always doubting what we do or are about to do. It is the part we call our Ego, always casting dispersions, always creating uncertainty, making us feel a little crazy at times, drawing on and living off the drama within the grit that enters our world . . . our shell.

Our Ego is not a part of our solar plexus, our reasoning and decision-making center. It is not part of the Voice that brings us Wisdom from our Ancient One, our Inner Child, to show us the way. It resides in our mind and is a combination of learned opinions and information that causes us to doubt ourselves, sometimes frequently, sometimes less. It is this doubt that we need to learn how to make quiet, and even non-existent, turning up the volume on the Voice that works together with our solar plexus.

The doubting Ego has no place on our Soul's path. It is not interested in us becoming the best version of our self. It wants us to stay safe within the world of other's opinions, not risking ridicule or rejection, always craving acceptance and praise. It constantly strives for and feeds on the limiting and jumbled opinions of others. Sadly, there are those people who do not want us to succeed more than they have, and this means that those people are governed by their Ego and not their Soul.

**The key to overcoming the Ego, consumed by so many opinions, is *self-belief*.**

To believe in our self is to trust our inner Voice, our Inner Child with the Warrior within, using the feeling at the center of our solar plexus to guide us with each step that we take on our path; a journey that cannot be guided by the Ego hence the opinions of others, but rather the Soul that lies within.

We are here to serve our Purpose in life which cannot be guided by thousands of others. We can only be guided by all parts true to ourselves, our heart and our Soul. Our mind, usually governed by our Ego, must be a part that *co-operates* with all other parts, moving together in unison to achieve the same ultimate goal and to be the best version of our self living our Soul Purpose, always listening to our Voice and making decisions with our gut, staying on our path, achieving peace and happiness, and feeling free.

*All* of this is fuelled by *self-belief*. Without this vital fuel, we cannot facilitate all parts that make us whole. Our Soul dwindles and we cannot hear our Voice of Wisdom. If the Ego controls the mind, filling it with the insignificant opinions of others, we become like everyone else and we lose our uniqueness . . . our Soul . . . and our Purpose in life.

But if we hold onto our self-belief, trusting the Voice inside and our gut instincts, we continue to thrive in what becomes a wonderful world of excitement and happiness, free from the opinions of others that we tend to use as validation of our self-worth. Only we need to validate ourselves by using the positive feelings that we feel as a *gauge of happiness*. When we reach our goals within our Soul Purpose and see the positive effects they have on others (not the controlling negative affects), this is then a *true gauge of success*.

So it is important to note that our success can only be measured by not only how we feel but how we make others feel, that being happy, motivated, loved, and supported, especially when *they choose* to listen to their own Voice. All those emotions then combine to help them feel much better about themselves, giving them hope and motivation to change for their highest good, fuelling their own self-belief. This then becomes another ripple effect of love, kindness, and goodness, enriching your wellbeing as well as someone else's, the ultimate level of success. This is what it's all about and ultimately starts with you and your Inner Child, with the Warrior within keeping you strong to stay true to yourself and who you are. Stay strong, listen to your Voice, trust your gut instincts . . . believe in yourself. You can't help but succeed.

Yet, why is self-belief such a major dilemma with many people? Because we are so caught up with social-media, self-image and the need to 'fit in' therefore we have lost touch with our ability to propel our own confidence and just be our self when others are around us. We have lost the ability to simply try and do what makes us happy, what 'lights us up' from the inside, what generates excitement and ecstasy in our very Core . . . just like when we were a child. We did not really care too much about what most people thought. We were too enthralled with the magic of Nature and the excitement of new experiences. And if we laughed until our sides hurt, this was the icing on the cake.

We are so awkward when it comes to believing in our selves because we have forgotten how to take risks and simply enjoy life for all it has to experience. We are scared to be our self and to just be happy, yet this is what life is all about. This is where we need to make a *change*. We just need to *believe* that we can. We just need to stop and Breathe.

# 7 JUST BREATHE

There is a place that we need to find and go to when we are feeling overwhelmed with indecision and lack of direction. It is a place deep inside our Core that takes us away from the buzz and the noise of the outer world which bombards us with too many insignificant opinions not related to our spiritual destiny, our Soul Purpose.

This place is quiet and serene and is the safest place we can go to. It is where our Inner Child stays, and also where our Ancient One can be found to confirm all that we need to know. We are warm and safe here always because this is *home*, not so much in a physical sense but in a deep and profound spiritual sense. This is where *change* happens for our wellbeing.

To get to this place we need to stop and focus on the present - the Now. We can't dwell in the past nor can we worry about what is to come in the future. When we go there we may also need to find a quiet place, if possible, in our physical surroundings. Most importantly we need to find somewhere where we are removed from the opinions of others so that the messages we receive from our Voice are clear and concise to reduce confusion. By doing this we are also able to focus on our breathing.

Our breath is so crucial in the process of connecting to our inner parts of Wisdom. It allows us to slow down and to be present in the Now. As we close our eyes in our quiet space away from others, we can focus on our breath slowly and deeply entering into our body and being released, continually finding ourselves in a state of calm and peace with every breath, opening our heart, our solar plexus and quieting our mind . . . our Ego. As we continue to breathe and stay focused on our breath, we continue to move into our Core, our place of quietness and serenity, our place of safety right in the very center of our self . . . our being. It is here where the answers to our questions reside. It is here where we can hear our Voice, and it is here where we can feel our gut instinct and the vibration of our Soul within our heart. It is here where all our parts of self unite and become connected to guide us through our journey with each step we take and at every crossroad. It is here where we learn to trust and believe in ourselves. It is here where we take the grit and turn it into a *Pearl*.

Our breath is so important in finding our quiet and special place. Without the stillness of just breathing, we will not connect to our Soul, our Wisdom, and so we continue to be baffled by the calamity of the outside world, caught up in the rush, never stopping to hear our Voice that is always at the ready with further advice or instructions. All we need to do is stop, breathe, ask and listen.

Breathing connects us to our life force energy, connecting us to every cell in our body and every part. It is what keeps us alive. It is our breath that unites all parts physically, mentally and spiritually.

**It is our Breath that nourishes our Soul
especially amongst the stillness of the Now.**

We cannot survive amongst the constant chaos of the outside world without consulting our inner world of parts that hold the answers of amazing brilliance. Those moments that we feel are "Aha!" moments, where amazing epiphanies rise to the surface of our consciousness with a brilliant flash of light, causing an explosion of excitement and happiness in our Core . . . our gut and our heart. These moments come to us in the stillness when we just stop and just breathe, causing a chain reaction of parts to connect inside us in order for this magical moment to happen. This is the moment when our Ancient One awakens, the Voice is activated, the Wisdom is presented to us and the light bulb within our mind's eye shines brightly.

This 'connection' is so central and so amazing as it allows us to strengthen our belief system, especially when that 'light bulb moment' becomes a reality. We increase our self- esteem and our resilience to try new things every time we achieve our goals and our dreams.

Every step, every motion forward is crucial to maintaining and upholding our self-belief that we can achieve whatever we put our minds to. And of course, we are able to come to the realization that we are capable of so much more than we could ever initially conceive. We are full of ideas and inspiration. No one has the power to take any of our inspiration and creativity away or to stifle our progress.

If we continue to stay on our path and just believe that we can make it, we <u>will</u> make it. We are the captain of our ship. We just have to know our ship well, down to every last nut and bolt, and all that it can do, pushing it to its limits and past all expectations so that we can discover new parts, new talents and gifts, and new horizons. After all, a boat is not meant to stay onshore. There is too much to see, too much to explore and many, many adventures to be had. We are all explorers on our unique journey full of continuous light bulb moments.

All we have to do is take another breath and hold onto self-belief as we take that first bold step forward towards making another light bulb moment happen, one after another, and ultimately fulfilling our Purpose. We just have to Breathe.

# 8 SIGNS POINT THE WAY

Sometimes it can be difficult to hear our Inner Voice or to understand just what it is our gut instinct has to say. The Ego, our critical mind, fills us with doubt and fear, muddling the messages we receive internally. This can happen quite frequently for we are only human. We cannot be expected to be perfect as we are on a journey of constant learning. It is during these times of confusion that we need to pay attention to our surroundings, where the answer to our questions may lie.

Remembering the story of Buddha (the enlightened one), the King's son Siddhartha could not be withheld from the Signs of the Universe and was inevitably exposed to these Signs that were drawing him to follow his Wisdom and his path to later become Buddha. Obviously, not all of us are destined to become Buddha, but it is within our surroundings, if we pay close enough attention to all details, that we may also receive a Sign from the Universe, our Creator, that will help us to ignore the confusing chatter of our mind, our Ego, and to get back on track with following our path.

There are times when we do need to seek guidance from the Universe because sometimes the next step on our path can be daunting and unknown territory. We can get so caught up with making sure that our next move is the *right* one, and with making sure we action it *perfectly*, that we become frozen, unable to make that next decision. We lose connection with our Voice, our Ancient One, and are unable to gain any clarity or Wisdom. It can become a blur of extreme emotions such as fear, anxiety, frustration or even disappointment. We become overwhelmed with our doubting Ego.

This is the moment when we need to take the initiative and feel free to ask God, Source or even the Angels (whatever your belief) for a solution to our question or dilemma, whether it is to do with our next step or even how to deal with a difficult person that has caused us to stop in our tracks. We just simply need to ask the question, out loud or in our minds, and ask that a Sign be shown that we will *understand* as being our answer.

There are so many ways in which we are given Signs. It can be within Nature, just as the Ancient People would have received them long ago, or it could even be in the words of a song. You could see a sign on TV or on social media, or you could hear it in a conversation, whether it be yours or someone else's. No matter how the Sign is delivered, if it resonates with your Core, your heart and Soul, as being a Sign then this is your answer and your guidance.

Some say this is merely superstition, but the Ancient People have been using Signs for many generations. They have always looked to Nature for answers including weather patterns, sightings of certain birds or animals that may cross their path, and many more. Signs are not uncommon in their world and you will come to realize that Signs are very much all around us all the time if you just take the time to look and listen.

Sometimes we don't even have to ask any questions to receive a Sign of encouragement, that wink from the Universe that we are doing great and we are going the right way. If we are following our 'true north', our Soul Purpose, those Signs will continue to appear like breadcrumbs on our path.

Some Signs might be as simple as a rainbow which may appear in the sky, or from a sunbeam passing through a pane of glass, or a picture in a magazine. No matter how it appears it is still a Sign, especially if you notice rainbows often. They are a Sign of hope and not to give up.

Some people may be drawn to feathers on the ground which can mean the Universe, your angels or guides are helping you at that point in time. Whatever your belief, this guidance is sure to be from a place of love and compassion.

It doesn't matter what the Sign is or how it is delivered to you, as long as it means *something* to you then this is all that matters. There is no right or wrong. All Signs are for each person and open to interpretation by that person. If it touches your heart and Soul, if it gives you an "A-ha!" moment, then this is the answer that you have been waiting for.

Sometimes we might feel that we have missed our Sign because we have not seen it or felt it was the right one. This may be because we may not have asked the right or a *genuine* question, that being a question from our heart and not from our Ego. This is when we need to go into our Core to *feel* the right question, asking whether the question improves our wellbeing and leads us closer to our Purpose?

> "Do I need to change my circle of friends to improve my happiness and self-confidence?"
>
> "Do I have to go to University and get a degree in Medicine?"
>
> "Is this job going to light me up and help me to get closer to my Soul Purpose?"

**If we ask a genuine, heart-felt question then the Universe will continue to show us Signs until we 'get it'.**

So if you keep seeing beautiful butterflies flitting by, be sure to know that you are on the road to self-transformation. Just like the butterfly, when we feel we are in a dark place and surrounded by change, we just have to have faith that we will emerge with more Wisdom, adding to our own wings of beauty and uniqueness. We don't always have to 'know' the next step but it is reassuring to know that the Universe will always guide us when we feel isolated and lost.

Rest assured, to be aware of and take heed of the messages within the Signs around us does not indicate our weakness of not hearing our inner Wisdom. Instead, it shows an awakening to the energy that is all around us and our ability to tune into it. It shows humility and the ability to not just serve ourselves but also the Universe, for this is where these Signs have come from in the first place. Noticing these Signs not only heightens our awareness but also brings back our Voice . . . our self-belief. They point the way to reveal who we are, our path . . . our Soul Purpose.

**Signs bring us back to our inner self so that we can begin to trust our Voice and instincts once again, giving us confidence and strengthening our Self-Belief.**

# 9 TRUST YOURSELF

There are often so many twists and turns in the road we sometimes lose our strength to keep balance and continue hoping not to fall in fear of humiliation, hurt and even betrayal. We come to realize that these twists and turns are somewhat continuous and it can sometimes be a struggle to keep standing.

When we travel a convoluted and bumpy road, we need to dig deep to find the courage and strength to keep going. These times can be so difficult and can bring mental, physical and emotional pressure, exhaustion and sometimes even pain. There is always a way to pass any obstacle no matter how difficult or how impossible it may seem. So many times we become daunted by the apparent mountain that appears before us, wondering just how we are going to conquer it this time. We start to become very uneasy, nervous, tense, sweaty palms, a rise in body temperature. We then lose sight of everything around us, become uncertain in our thinking and panic sets in. It's all overwhelming and so confusing when we don't take the time to properly analyze the situation and jump straight into a "fight-flight" reaction.

**It's all about Trust, knowing that the way to conquer any obstacle will come to us . . . if we *let* it.**

We need to do our very best to remain calm and become focused on our breathing, slowing it down so we can process all the bits of information that are before us. Making sure we have all the information might require us to ask questions (so that we don't habitually take the easy road of simply accepting the opinions of others), which then allows us to investigate further so we are able to properly *digest* the situation. This then allows us to go deeper into our Core being, allowing our Voice to be heard and drawing from the Wisdom of our Ancient One where the true solution can be found.

We don't need to be some kind of *genius* with a huge IQ to solve any sort of problem. We need to trust that if we provide ourselves with as much information to the problem as possible, the difficult situation at hand, this will then allow us to find the true answer that will resonate with our gut and with our Soul.

The more we practice this process the better we get at it, and the faster we get at reaching the solution. This then leads to a greater sense of *self-belief* that we can work things out ourselves, using our gut instinct to weigh up the validity of the information or opinions given to our questions.

**From this greater sense of Self Belief also comes a sense of *strength and power*.**

We all need to be aware of how much the information that is swirling around us can affect us in either a positive or a negative way. We need to use our internal barometer, our gut instinct, to sift and sort through it all and choose only that which will empower us in a 'healthy' way.

We empower ourselves when we not only reach a solution but more so when we receive confirmation from a positive outcome that our solution works. This moment of triumph boosts our self-confidence to higher levels, helping us to be more resilient the next time we face difficulty, and helping us to face these hard times of pressure with renewed confidence in our ability to conquer what now appears to be a smaller mountain.

And we have the power to conquer and achieve if we stop, breathe, assess the situation and listen to our Voice of Wisdom. We can always find an answer . . . a solution . . . if we stop *reacting* and just *listen*.

You are so powerful in so many ways. There is so much force within you to conquer your greatest challenges and your biggest fears. We all have our demons to face whether big or small. We all have those moments of feeling overwhelmed, anxious, tired or even angry when things just don't seem to be working out. So we become so annoyed and frustrated with the whole situation that it is just so easy to just give up. This is the moment where you need to dig so very deeply and find the lesson within the situation.

"What is it teaching me?"

"What is it that I need to do to conquer this mountain and overcome my fear to do so?"

"What tools can I use that I have used before, or maybe I can learn from someone else to give me an advantage to finding a solution?"

"What Wisdom can I use, from all that I have done and achieved, that will help me get to the other side and feel at peace again?"

We all have the ability to use our gathered or innate Wisdom, to move forward and achieve great things no matter how big or small. Don't be afraid to *trust yourself*. Your answers are the truest and purest because they come from the Ancient One and are for your highest wellbeing and Purpose.

# 10 COMPLETE HARMONY

When things seem to be going wrong and it all becomes frustrating and overwhelming at times, it means that all our parts are out of sync, not communicating or integrating with each other so that we can function optimally. We lose our sense of freedom and tranquility, getting lost amongst the turmoil and disharmony. Nothing appears to be going right and sometimes there seems to be no end to this endless line of mishaps and non-events.

There comes a time when we must realize and understand that these negative events are our creation, the story we have pre-written in our minds somewhere along our path and they have become, for some moment in time, the vision of intense focus. It comes back to the old saying: "Be careful what you wish for!"

When we dwell on the negative events in our life and attach them to negative emotions, the emotion brings this negative memory to life as it continues to feed it more and more with negative emotion; whether it is anger, sadness, guilt or fear. The negative emotion then consumes us, lowering our positive vibration that we usually emit to the Universe especially when we are happy, calm and even exited, and then transforms the positive into a negative vibration. If this negative vibration, caused by continuous negative thoughts and emotions, continues for even a few minutes, the negative vibration that we emit begins to attract more negative events and emotions because in the world of quantum physics . . . *like attracts like.*

It is very important to notice our negative emotions and try to trace them back to the thoughts that have been passing through our mind, our ever burdensome Ego. Then we can acknowledge these thoughts, process why we feel the way we do about them and let them go because hanging onto these negative emotions causes disharmony in our mental, physical and spiritual parts. If held for too long, months or years, they begin to show up as disease, that is Dis-Ease. For example, anxiety, depression, organ failure, cancer, etc.

Dwelling on the negative goes against the Principles of Life. We cannot survive (Principal 1) or function with so much negativity causing disharmony within all parts of our being. It is difficult to project love, understanding, patience, kindness, and compassion (Principle 2) or forgiveness (Principle 3) when we are projecting so much anger, hate, guilt, and fear. And lastly, our ability to achieve acceptance (Principle 4) of all that we are is riddled with holes and becomes so disconnected when we are overwhelmed by so much negativity.

Even though we cannot suppress our emotions, nor ignore the event or memory that is causing us so much negativity and internal disharmony, it is important to acknowledge the *threat* to our positive vibration and *all* the emotions that come with it. We need to find our special place of solitude and breathe as we continue the process of acknowledging this event, or string of events, continuing to recognize the emotions that stem from it. By doing this we are able to process all the information using our gut instinct and our inner Wisdom as to what is valid and what is based on the insignificant opinions of others.

By dissecting the information it becomes more of a scientific process that is less emotionally charged, and begins the process of turning an emotionally negative memory into just grit, a piece of annoyance and aggravation. We need to analyze just why these emotions have occurred and the lesson to be learned. We need to go deep into our Core to understand that this grit, now a negative and re-occurring memory, can only hurt us *if we let it*. But if we discover the lesson that we need to learn from this memory to better ourselves, we have changed what was negative into a *positive*. We have taken the grit that has entered our world, removed the attached negative emotion and improved our reaction to it by attaching or coating it with further information. This makes the memory a more valuable item to refer to and to take on your travels along your path . . . your journey.

**What was a negative memory, an aggravating piece of grit, has been transformed into a valuable lesson . . . a valuable Pearl.**

The more lessons we can recognize and then continue to nurture the information within, the richer we become for we are expanding our experience and ultimately our Wisdom, which is knowing how to deal with the grit that enters our special place, dissect and remove the emotion, see the lesson for what it is and cultivate it into a Pearl, a valuable fragment of knowledge.

And our vibration starts to return to one of positivity.

So we learn the lesson and then shift our focus onto thoughts of what we do want, thoughts of what will bring us happiness, excitement, tranquility and most importantly thoughts of events that fill us with Love, the highest positive vibration of them all. By shifting our thoughts to what fills us with positive emotions changes our chemical composition to one of positivity and we begin to attract more of what we are focusing on, that being more positive events and more positive emotions. Again, like attracts like.

As we fill up with positive emotions, our parts become in sync with each other, helping us to relax and hear our Voice and Wisdom with such clarity that we continue on our path in *complete harmony*.

# 11 CREATING YOUR STORY WITH GRATITUDE

So if like attracts like, it is suffice to say: Everything we think and everything we say, if felt with deep emotion, is energy transferred into action and it appears in our life. It may not happen overnight, although in some instances it can, but eventually it does happen.

There is so much we can create in our lives just by a simple thought. When this thought is accompanied by emotion it accelerates the occurrence of this thought into the Now. Even when things go wrong, we tend to blame outside forces for what is happening to us rather than take responsibility for what we have created.

**Whatever we think we create.**

So we must think of positive thoughts to attract positive scenarios of what we would like to happen and attach to these scenarios just how we think we would feel, for example happy, excited, peaceful, thankful . . . as if it *did* happen. Most importantly, we need to thank the Universe or God in *advance* for this wonderful scenario as if it has already happened.

> **It's all about *the positive emotion coupled with gratitude*
> that brings your wishes and dreams to fruition,
> creating the story that you want yourself to be a part of.**

We have the ability to manifest our deepest wishes, our deepest desires into reality. Our mind is a very powerful tool and if we can convince it (our Ego) to believe that this is how it should be, that this dream or goal is our reality, then this energy or vibration that we are projecting to the Universe can only be matched with all factors and variables that will be attracted to us to make it our reality, our Story.

> **These wishes must come from the heart and be part of your Soul's Path and Purpose for it to become reality. It needs to be from the depths of your Inner Child and your Ancient One, to benefit your highest good.**

Even the words we use from day to day have a massive impact on the story we create. If we use negative or derogatory words, especially about ourselves, we vibrate at a lower frequency and attract the very thing that we don't want. When we use positive and uplifting words, we increase our vibration to a much higher and positive frequency, attracting all the positive and good things that we want in our lives.

Words are always a part of the story we create for ourselves. We should always be wary of not only the words we use but the words we dwell on, especially negative words that we are playing over and over in our heads, linking us to the story that we are living now.

> *"I am not smart enough to . . ."*
>
> *"I am not fast enough to . . ."*
>
> *"I am not good enough for . . ."*

These same words shape our beliefs about ourselves. So it is important not only to use words that are positive, but also words that are full of love, support and compassion, especially when they start with "I am . . .".

> "I am great at . . ."
>
> "I am beautiful."
>
> "I am clever."
>
> "I am enough."
>
> "I am worthy."

These words, when positive, have such a calming and peaceful effect on our Inner Child and Ancient One, nurturing us from the inside out.

We also need to use peaceful and loving words not only to ourselves but to others, creating yet another ripple effect of positive vibrations. It is so very important to extend such words further than ourselves so that this ripple effect comes back to us creating an overlap of endless positivity, love, and compassion.

There is such a great deal of importance on how we say things. We know that the words we choose to use affects the energy that we project. However, it is the <u>intention</u> behind those words that is the major decider as to whether they emit positive or negative energy, which in turn makes them either beneficial or harmful, true or false. That is when our barometer, our gut instinct, kicks in to help us determine not only what words are negative or positive, but whether those people we choose to surround ourselves with are positive or negative also, and whether they are beneficial or detrimental to our wellbeing.

When we are in tune with our gut instinct and our heart, we will feel the need to shy away from people who continue to talk negatively and use derogatory words as it negatively affects *our* vibration. Instead, we instinctively seek those who speak positively to raise our vibration to much more positive levels.

This also includes TV programs, movies, and music that we expose ourselves to. Anything that shows or talks about violence and negativity we recognize as being uncomfortable, quite harmful and even toxic to our senses. We also begin to reject various types of toxic social media as they no longer resonate with the higher vibration that our Inner Child and Ancient One are trying to achieve. The discomfort ultimately becomes too much for us to bear. Uplifting TV programs, movies, and music are more soothing to our senses, and their positive energy or vibes are resonating with us for our wellbeing.

Over time, listening to negative news reports, or negative people in our lives, is no longer of any importance and becomes too harsh for us to pay attention to. We come to realize they are no longer necessary and choose to cut them out of our life. They are no longer necessary inclusions to our Story.

**Every word we say, every thought we think, whatever we focus on becomes our reality, the Story that we alone create for ourselves.**

Stay true to the goodness of your heart and the words that surround you will always be full of goodness too. It can be no other way. This is physics.

# 12 STAND YOUR GROUND

Every day we come into contact with the insignificant opinions of others whether it is our friends, family or people we don't know. Their opinions, that is their words and energies, can make our gut turn or make us feel bad for listening to our Voice and our heart, for following the Dream deep down inside us as we travel our path and fulfill our Soul Purpose.

This Dream is what gives us hope, inspiration and the will to keep moving forward to reach it. This Dream stems from the Core of who we are with our Inner Child and Ancient One, helping us to navigate our way one step at a time. Only you can understand the meaning of this Dream and the weight of its importance, as it was designed solely for the one person who carries it deep within their Soul . . . You.

**This Dream is the key that opens all the right doors, and will always be one of the most important and integral parts to all of our parts that make us who we are.**

Wellbeing comes from the happiness we experience as we continue to follow our path and keep our sights on the goal of reaching our Dream. It is a difficult road when we allow the opinions of others to sway us from our Dream, which could be many Dreams in our lifetime.

When we listen to the opinions of others just to please others and lessen our discomfort to just fit in, it becomes *more* of a burden. We stop listening to our Voice and our gut instinct starts to turn over and over inside, making us feel more uncomfortable within ourselves. Our happiness begins to disappear as we continue to seek the approval of others, constantly craving validation through others which then reaches an insatiable and unrealistic level of attainment. This causes our emotions to become negative, such as sadness and even depression, when we don't get that validation.

Living off and craving the opinions of others is dangerous and addictive. It silences our Voice, reduces our ability to trust our gut instinct and we then ignore our Inner Child and Ancient One, our true source of information and guidance that leads us to fulfill our Dreams, our Purpose; where only our true happiness and confidence can be found, our true and constant source of *self-validation*.

We need to be strong and self-sufficient. We need to ignore those insignificant opinions of others that go against what we truly believe inside us is good for our wellbeing.

**We need to stand our ground, push forward
and fight for what we truly believe in.**

Imagine you are standing in a room surrounded by 50 people, some people you do know and some faces you don't recognize at all. Continue to imagine this room full of people talking *at you*, telling you what you should and shouldn't do. It becomes overwhelming not knowing who to listen to let alone who to believe. All you want to do is cover your ears and close your eyes to block them out. And blocking them out is effectively what we need to do when life reaches this point of utter confusion.

There is so much 'white noise', so much static and clutter that continues to bombard us from day to day. We can often struggle to turn down the volume let alone try to turn it off. We cannot seem to hear our Voice over it, our reasoning and gut instinct. It all becomes so loud and baffling, leaving us motionless and lost, unable to follow our path and pursue our dreams.

Even though we love and care for our friends and family, and they too sometimes offer us advice because they also care for our wellbeing, ultimately the decision is ours to make when we come to the crossroads of having to make a choice. We know deep down inside when we are making a good choice, that is a choice that is good for our wellbeing and is not harmful to others. On the flip side, we also know deep down when we are making a bad choice, a choice that is harmful to our wellbeing and sometimes to others.

Bad choices are usually fuelled and propelled by the insignificant opinions of others and a need to fit in and be approved of, for example drinking, smoking, being mean to and or excluding others.

**Good choices are created from within and are fuelled and propelled from love, compassion and the Wisdom within.**

If we stay true to who we are, always digging deep within ourselves as to whether the advice or the opinions of others are good or bad for us, we will *always* make the right choice. And if we look for the Signs around us as to whether we are headed in the right direction with the choices that lay before us, we have a better chance of staying on our path, continuing our journey of fulfilling our Dreams.

Life is always about making choices. Everything that comes before us is either a 'Yes' or a 'No'. If we listen closely to our Voice and the Wisdom within, we will *know* which answer to choose.

We need to believe in our self, abide by the 4 Principles of Life, collect and nurture our pearls, and *stand our ground*. This is the core of our Journey to fulfill our Life Purpose, always burning like a candle within your Soul and lighting the way.

# 13 SACRED SPACE

Ancient people from long ago were always in tune with themselves and their surroundings, including each other. They were able to use their senses to determine if things were good or bad, beneficial or harmful. They were able to able to hear their inner Voice with such precision, such clarity, staying in tune with themselves and with Nature, so they could not only survive but be prepared for what was to come.

Unfortunately, we have lost the ability to stay in tune with ourselves and also with Nature, always looking for outside information and advice. We have lost the ability to be self-sufficient in so many ways that we continue to get lost and confused, not knowing which step to take next and losing our path along the way.

We have become quite dependent on the opinions of others and will often take on board that idea or solution that belongs to the majority. We can't seem to use our inner Wisdom, so full of inspiration and creativity, just so eager for us to listen and to succeed.

We have disabled ourselves on so many levels because we are afraid to be different, that we won't fit in and ultimately be rejected from the group that we want to be a part of, always looking for their approval to feed our sense of worthiness. This, in turn, is unhealthy on so many different levels, especially when it comes to our self-belief.

We are so equipped to make our own decisions. We have so many gifts and tools within us to create our happiness and our strength. We have so much inner Wisdom accessible from so many generations before us and we have it all inside our Sacred Space.

We know just by stopping, breathing and asking our genuine question that we can go into this place with no criticism or judgment. We have our Power inside this space to be able to be free and consider all information without being pushed or rushed to make a decision.

It is here that we can use our barometer, our gut instinct, to determine what is good and what is not good, what is beneficial or what is harmful.

It is here that we decide what is true to our identity of self and what is false.

It is here where we decide if the information is part of our self-belief system or if it is not.

This last decision is so very critical because it can enable us or disable us. It all depends on what we choose to keep and what we don't. We can choose to keep positive, uplifting and motivating information or we can choose that which will harm and even sabotage us. We have the power to *choose* in our Sacred Space what we nurture and what we wish to create to be a part of our Story.

When it comes to the advice of others, some advice is given by those driven by their Soul and can be good for our well being and Purpose. Some are driven by their Ego and their advice can push us off course, leaving us consumed with more fear and uncertainty.

So how do we know which advice is beneficial and which is insignificant?

It all comes down to our gut instinct, whether we feel comfortable and even excited about the advice given, or totally uncomfortable with our stomach churning over and over leaving us unable to take that next step forward because we are surrounded by doubt and fear. We cannot ignore those feelings inside our solar plexuses, always present with every conversation we have . . . with every step we take. We cannot ignore our barometer that grows stronger and louder, urging us to go into our special place . . . our Love . . . our Sacred Space to take heed to our Inner Voice and the Wisdom of our Ancient One always at the ready.

Time to listen and time to breathe is crucial when we are in a state of confusion and misunderstanding with the advice or information presented to us. We need to go to our *Sacred Space* to ensure we have properly digested it all, re-affirming our gut instinct of whether or not what we are being told resonates with who we are and why we are here.

Everything we are told can either form a part of our internal belief system or is discarded. It all depends on how strong our connection is to our Inner Child who knows us so well . . . or how dominating our fear-driven Ego is.

Our belief system is fuelled by these two opposing forces, continually battling it out as to which one will add to this unlimited tank of positive and negative beliefs. The more we listen to our insecure Ego, the more this tank is filled with irregular, unsubstantiated and negative beliefs which are self-limiting and self-sabotaging. As we continually play these negative beliefs over and over in our minds, we continue to reinforce our supposed limitations and unworthiness. We become stuck, unfulfilled, unhappy, depressed, angry, aggressive . . . living a sad, negative and uneventful life.

The more we listen to our Inner Child of endless Wisdom, the more we process our gut feelings, processing what information or advice we are given (wanted or unwanted), growing our belief system with properly digested, accepted and nurtured information, and the more we develop and evolve within our Sacred Space.

All information, all Signs, all feelings are continually sifted through, processed and sorted, resulting in keeping only that which is significant to our Soul Purpose and our wellbeing. This is why this place is so *sacred*. We cannot afford to let in anything negative, detrimental or toxic. We cannot misalign ourselves from who we truly are, taking away our freedom and our happiness.

We must fuel our belief system, our tank, with motivation and excitement, with goodness and many Pearls. We cannot fill it with rubbish that being the harmful, insignificant opinions of others that do not resonate with nor should enter our Sacred Space. We must continue to stay strong, despite the bombardment of information and advice, rejecting what *feels* so wrong and accepting what lifts us higher and even higher. This then becomes our belief system . . . our *Truth*.

**We are what we make ourselves to be.**

We are solely responsible for how this "process" takes place. We can either make it a process, a journey, that is full of pain and hardship, or one that is full of joy and fulfillment. Again, this process is about the choices we make - 'accept' or 'reject', 'Yes' or 'No'. We have the power to choose and to *choose well* if we use the tools, the Wisdom, the guidance we were born with, all accessible in our Sacred Space.

Once we free ourselves from the negative and focus on something positive, we start to find more and more positive opinions that continue to resonate with our Soul, bringing us closer to our heart space, our Sacred Space, where we start to hear our Voice, our gut instinct, our heartbeat, as we go deeper and deeper inside ourselves accumulating all bits of positive information, feeling the resonance of what is *true* now building inside us. As we continue to breathe during this process of extracting the truth, extracting any negative emotions and feelings, the grit along the way, we coat them instead with valuable information of a lesson learned . . . our Pearl. We continue to nurture our Pearls and build from only what is positive, to fuel our strength and courage, continuing to empower ourselves for our highest wellbeing.

**Staying focused on the positive and allowing only the positive into our Sacred Space is all we need to feel good in the Now and move forward to fulfill our Dreams.**

We need to develop a thicker skin of armor, a thicker outer shell when it comes to the negative and insignificant opinions of others, and we must not allow these detrimental opinions, as well as the negative emotions that we attach to them, to enter into our Sacred Space. This space belongs to you and you only. You are the keeper of this Space and you have the absolute power to choose what can enter and what must remain outside. Again, it is a choice of either 'Yes' or 'No'.

And if you follow your instinct and listen to the Voice, your absolute tools for guidance, you will automatically know *what is not* to be accepted and *what is* to be accepted into your Sacred Space, continuing to nurture your heart and Soul.

As we look at everything that surrounds us as 'Yes' (feels good) or 'No' (feels bad) the sifting process becomes easier and easier until our Sacred Space is filled with positive feelings and thoughts creating a sense of peace, power and freedom . . . and a beautiful Story.

# 14 THE LIGHT OF COMPASSION

Where there is darkness we instinctively look for a glimmer of light for the darkness has always been something to fear and the light a place of hope. It is within these moments of darkness that we dig deep to find our greatest strength and resources, finding just how courageous and resilient we are in the face of adversity. Somehow we manage to find our way back to a place of hope and inspiration because we *believed* we could.

When we are surrounded by darkness and adversity we focus on our *senses*. We retreat to our fundamental resources when we can no longer rely on our 'sight'. We hear the urgency of our breathing, we feel the intensity of our heart beating and our body temperature rising, feeling the discomfort of beads of sweat on our forehead, underarms and the palms of our hands. These uncomfortable signals from our body are informing us that we are surrounded by negative energy that does not serve us favorably and is somewhat detrimental to our wellbeing. There is nothing wrong with feeling these sensations as this is our way of knowing that we need to take some sort of action to move away from the negativity surrounding us, our barometer in action. It is our body's way of alerting us that it's time to forge through the darkness of negativity and start looking for the light of positivity.

Something inside us always helps us to put one foot in front of the other no matter what is going on around us. We sense a surge of energy from the depths of our gut, driving us forward with every step, with every word we utter from our mouths. If we immediately listen to the Voice and Wisdom of the Ancient One we reach a solution at lightning speed and all is on the road to recovery. If we listen to the fear-based opinions of Ego we become instantly consumed by fear and even anger, saying and doing things that result in hurting someone else and eventually ourselves.

There is so much intensity and force when we are focused on hurting others that ultimately brings so much negativity back into our world. Of course, this brings more negativity and a vicious cycle of negative events supposedly deemed to be "bad luck". Now we know that this is not the case at all. It is a product of our harmful thoughts, our negative emotions and most definitely our ill intentions.

We must always say and do things from a place of peace and compassion (remembering Principle 2 in Chapter 4), despite that moment of hurt and frustration, as a positive response can only attract a positive result. To think otherwise is futile.

So it is important, during that moment of hurt and frustration, to go deep inside your Sacred Space as you breathe, to find your best solution at that point in time, even if the solution is to walk away so you can find a better solution later. We do not have to find a solution within the second or minute, especially when we are surrounded by white noise and chaos. We do have the choice to move away and find our Sacred Space, to consult our Ancient One and make the best decision for all concerned.

**The ultimate solution is one of compassion for not only others, but for yourself also, and this is the solution that will be the light through the darkness . . . the *Light of Compassion*.**

A solution with no compassion becomes a solution of greed and further intolerance which creates further disharmony, anxiety, fear, and anger. *Negativity breeds negativity.*

A solution based on compassion becomes a solution of peace and harmony for everyone. Without compassion, the light in our heart and Soul dies and we remain in total darkness and misery. The Light of Compassion is the only way to fuel our Souls and the positivity we wish to attract into our life, bringing us to our Life Purpose which is more fulfilling and has more meaning when it is fuelled by compassion.

# 15 SOME WHERE...

Somewhere there is going to be a place in time where we feel out of balance and totally unstable, not in control.

Somewhere there will be that moment when you will want to block out all the noise and confusion just to stop all the outside opinions from entering your Sacred Space, hoping to find peace and tranquility just for a sparing moment of the day.

And when this moment arrives you will know what to do, instantly connecting to the Voice within, calming you with Wisdom from the Ancient One . . . the Inner Child who loves you most. This will be your moment of triumph for you instinctively know how to believe in yourself despite the utter chaos that is swirling around you.

As you continue to go within your Sacred Space, you are drawing all that you need from an endless well of knowledge, the Pearls that you have collected and nurtured, continually evolving into a Warrior of Wisdom. There is no need for insignificant opinions to validate who you are. There is no need to continue to fuel your Ego's constant craving to be liked and to belong with people who don't believe in you, nor respect your Dreams or Soul Purpose.

Your journey is of great importance to you as well as to those whose lives will change immensely in so many positive ways because of it. Do not doubt that what lies before you is of great importance. We are all here for a reason with a specific role to play in the wellbeing of others, whether it be people, children, animals, the environment. We all have special talents and gifts given to us to be shared with so many. Somewhere there is a bunch of souls that will need you to be the catalyst, improving their path and their wellbeing, ultimately creating one big ripple effect of improving the world around us.

Stay true to your heart and soul, walking the path you are meant to travel. Some roads will be rocky, some steep, some seemingly impossible to pass through. These are all lessons to be learned, Pearls to nurture and keep. Everything happens for a reason and as they say: "What doesn't kill you only makes you stronger."

Don't dwell on the negative. Find the lesson within. Go deep within your Sacred Space to find a way, the Voice that carries so much Wisdom, support and compassion, giving you the solution to turn it into a positive . . . . an amazing Pearl . . . attracting more positive. You and only you have the power to take the very first step in making a change that will push you, if only 1 degree, in a totally different direction. This slight *shift,* however many times it happens in a lifetime, creates a different pattern of behavior, a different outcome, a different Story.

Just follow the Signs when you ask for directions from the Universe, when your Voice doesn't seem to be clear. Never doubt that the solution or directions along your path will present themselves. All you have to do is *ask*. And when you are *ready* to open up to the possibilities of what the answer is, it may take 1 minute, 1 day, 1 week or so . . . when your mind is free from constant, insignificant chatter and opinions, your answer will come to you. Your gut will instinctively know, with a sureness that resonates so strongly with every part of your being, that the step you are about to take is definitely the right one.

And even if that step is one of trepidation because the waters before you are rough, frightening, deep, dark seas or waves 100 feet high, know that this moment will pass and you will come out the other side with yet another lesson learned, another Pearl, more Wisdom, more confidence and another step closer on your Soul Purpose, to your Dream.

The Universe would not have given this path to you if it did not think you have what it takes to complete your mission on this Earth. It is an adventure worth exploring and enjoying without the opinions of others and our negative Ego running and ruining it all.

*Somewhere you will shake and cry.*

*Somewhere you will face and conquer your fears.*

*Somewhere you will jump and scream with joy and pride.*

Somewhere you will achieve that ultimate sense of accomplishment and success because you stuck it out to the very end to make a difference, followed your path and fulfilled your Dream.

Somewhere you will say or do something from the heart, with compassion and kindness, to help raise the positive vibration of another person.

Somewhere there will be that person that travelled along the road beside you for that moment in time, be it 1 minute, 1 hour, 1 week, 1 year . . . who helped raised your vibration from a place of compassion and kindness to one of positivity to create that 1 degree shift, helping you to reach your Dream. For they too are sharing their talents and gifts, helping you to remain positive with each step you take, helping you to stay true to who you are . . . a beautiful Soul, a Warrior of Wisdom fighting for what you believe in . . . your Dream.

# 16 YOUR PEARL, YOUR WORLD

Time is all we have when it comes to moving forward with our Purpose, our Dream. However, we cannot be too focused on the past because we cannot change it. We can only learn from it. Time cannot be a measurement of where we have been; only our memories and experience can do this. Time becomes irrelevant.

We do need to look in front of us when we travel along the road of our path. However, we cannot pre-empt what will happen on this path as there are too many variables, too many event happenings and people who cross our path, that continue to change its course from time to time, even though we somehow still end up reaching our end goal. Yes, we do use our intuition to guide us and to avoid certain detrimental and dangerous obstacles. But sometimes there are some obstacles and situations that are unavoidable, good or bad. These are the lessons we are meant to learn. Sometimes we just need to endure a bit of pain, a bit of grit, so that the lesson becomes meaningful, a Pearl that is ingrained in our DNA and becomes a part of our Wisdom.

So it is pointless to focus too much on the future. It is easier to focus on the Now, allowing life to unfold like a series of surprises. If we focus on the Now then we focus on *how much* we enjoy life's surprises, taking in the moment, using all our senses just like when we were a child, when time had no meaning and was totally irrelevant. We just enjoyed the moment and every moment of each day.

This is why our childhood memories are so clear and so vivid. Full of emotion and oozing with how we experienced them with every one of our 5 senses just like it was yesterday.

Remember when summer holidays felt like months on end, every day rolling into the next one. Every day seemed like an adventure. From the moment you woke up you could smell the scent of summer followed by the smell of breakfast. Running around in your brightly colored cotton clothes was so comfortable and bare feet was a pre-requisite from sun-up to sun-down. Soft green grass under your feet at the beginning of summer was so grounding.

These are the memories that our Inner Child collects to the very last detail. All the emotions and sensory feelings that are experienced at that moment are so strongly attached. It stays in our heart and becomes deeply embedded in our Soul, always a part of our DNA, our Ancient One, all experiences a lesson whether good or bad, all a part of our collection of Pearls.

We often have that feeling or memory being somewhere or doing something before, though quite often we can't pinpoint where along the timeline it actually occurred. Maybe it was this lifetime, maybe it was during another, but for some reason it is strongly familiar because it has been stored in our Soul's memory, our Wisdom from long ago still with us now. We will always continue to have these memories re-surfacing, triggered by a familiar sensory feeling that is occurring at that point in time, all of which contribute to who we are and adding to our uniqueness. We are full of memories and lessons that continue to guide us through life, helping us to make our 'Yes' or 'No' choices. We continue to add to them as we grow becoming a **Warrior of Wisdom**.

*Growth* can also give rise to our ability to make the most of every situation, good or bad. It is how we *choose* to see it and how we *choose* to interact with it, using our sensory feelings and emotions, which make a massive difference to how our Story is going to evolve before us.

As we reflect again on the oyster, one oyster can live amongst hundreds of other oysters on the side of a rock in the ocean. It manages to survive on the tides and currents of the ocean, going with the flow every day. Then a piece of grit or sand enters the oyster's shell, its Sacred Space, causing discomfort and irritability with the mollusk inside. For the mollusk to deal with this unwanted intrusion, the muscle uses its very special quality and gift to stop this piece of grit from harming it by producing layers of Nacre, leaving a hard outer pearly, rainbow exterior creating a beautiful Pearl.

We know that we too can create our own Pearl. When someone or something of annoyance enters our Sacred Space, we use our natural qualities, abilities, and gifts to protect ourselves and to turn this situation, which is causing us discomfort and grief, into a positive . . . a lesson . . . nurturing our Inner Wisdom . . . a Pearl.

This mere oyster, and so much in the world around us, is a part of the many Signs, messages, and lessons for us to grow and to enjoy the amazing journey along the way.

**You are the maker of your world. What you choose to do with the grit, and you do have a choice, will determine your world.**

Don't be afraid to grab the grit that enters your Space, your world, and turn it into a beautiful Pearl. After all . . . **No Grit, No Pearl**.

It is your world so be true to your heart, fulfill your Dreams . . . and may your Soul Journey be filled with many Pearls.

# ABOUT HELEN

Some would say I am a bit of a Jill-of-all-trades considering all the different positions I have had from administration, sales, real estate, interior design, natural healing therapies as well as having a degree in Psychology and being a mother of two to name a few!

With all my experience, there came a day when I realized that some jobs were not really 'me', and were the product of social conditioning as well as the multiple opinions and expectations of others. However, all were stepping stones with many lessons learned along the way, guiding me to this pivotal point. All my life I have been very intuitive and very connected to Spirit but, in reality, I had denied my true "essence" so I could just "fit in". . . somewhere.

Finally listening to Spirit (screaming at me by this point), I was drawn back into my Core with my Inner Child and where I remembered what it was that "lit me up", especially as a child . . . what came naturally from my heart and Soul. I loved to write and I loved to draw. And I felt the push to "Just start writing!". So I am extremely grateful to Spirit, to my inner Voice, my breathtaking Warrior as well as the Signs of encouragement along the way; including the amazing mushrooms that always appear in my garden to guide me. It's how and why this beautiful book of loving words and illustrations was created.

I hope this book has given you the courage and the confidence to nurture and strengthen your Inner Warrior, to follow your Dreams and to just be You.♥

**Next book in Warrior of Wisdom series:**

**Book 2 – Golden Ray Of Light**

www.ingramcontent.com/pod-product-compliance
Lightning Source LLC
Chambersburg PA
CBHW060818090426
42738CB00002B/34